zendoodle color

Calming Swirls

Stress-Relieving Designs to Color and Display

illustrations by

Nikolett Corley

ST. MARTIN'S GRIFFIN

NEW YORK

ZENDOODLE COLORING: CALMING SWIRLS.
Copyright © 2015 by St. Martin's Press. All rights reserved.
Printed in the United States of America. For information, address
St. Martin's Press, 175 Fifth Avenue, New York, N.Y. 10010.

www.stmartins.com

ISBN 978-1-250-08649-5 (trade paperback)

St. Martin's Griffin books may be purchased for educational, business, or promotional
use. For information on bulk purchases, please contact the Macmillan Corporate and
Premium Sales Department at 1-800-221-7945, extension 5442, or write to
specialmarkets@macmillan.com.

First Edition: August 2015

10 9 8 7 6 5 4

zendoodle coloring

Calming Swirls

Other great books in the series

zendoodle coloring

Creative Sensations

Enchanting Gardens

Inspiring Zendalas